LEADERSHIP
DEVELOPMENT GROUP

INSIGHTS INTO ACTION

Copyright 2014 by Jim Peal, Ph.D.

ISBN: 978-1511780636

April 2015

www.leadershipDG.com

"The ancestor of every action is a thought."
Ralph Waldo Emerson

2
www.leadershipDG.com

"Anything you build on a large scale or with intense passion invites chaos."
Francis Ford Coppola

3
www.leadershipDG.com

_____

_____

_____

_____

_____

_____

_____

_____

_____

_____

_____

_____

_____

_____

_____

_____

_____

_____

"Change before you have to."
Jack Welch

"I am enough of an artist to draw freely upon my imagination."
— Albert Einstein

LEADERSHIP
DEVELOPMENT GROUP

"A healthy attitude is contagious but don't wait to catch it from others. Be a carrier."
Tom Stoppard

"We choose our joys and sorrows long before we experience them."
— Kahlil Gibran

"I speak two languages, Body and English."
— Mae West

"Your present circumstances don't determine where you can go; they merely determine where you start."
Nido Qubein

"Your attitude toward life determines life's attitude towards you."
— John N. Mitchell

LEADERSHIP
DEVELOPMENT GROUP

"Chaos is the score upon which reality is written."
— Henry Miller

"Get your facts first, then you can distort them as you please."
— Mark Twain

"Adopting the right attitude can convert a negative stress into a positive one."
Hans Selye

"Common sense is genius dressed in its working clothes."
Ralph Waldo Emerson

_____

_____

_____

_____

_____

_____

_____

_____

_____

_____

_____

_____

_____

_____

_____

_____

_____

_____

"Who looks outside, dreams; who looks inside, awakes."
Carl Jung

"It is the mark of an educated mind to be able to entertain a thought without accepting it."
Aristotle

"Action speaks louder than words but not nearly as often."
Mark Twain

17
www.leadershipDG.com

"There is little difference in people, but that little difference makes a big difference. The little difference is attitude. The big difference is whether it is positive or negative."
W. Clement Stone

_____

_____

_____

_____

_____

_____

_____

_____

_____

_____

_____

_____

_____

_____

_____

_____

_____

"There is nothing so pitiful as a young cynic because he has gone from knowing nothing to believing nothing."
Maya Angelou

"Change is inevitable—except from a vending machine."
Robert C. Gallagher

"It takes but one positive thought when given a chance to survive and thrive to overpower an entire army of negative thoughts."
Robert H. Schuller

"The only disability in life is a bad attitude."
Scott Hamilton

"I've learned that people will forget what you said, people will forget what you did,
but people will never forget how you made them feel."
Maya Angelou
23
www.leadershipDG.com

"The moment there is suspicion about a person's motives, everything he does becomes tainted."
Gandhi

"Self-pity in its early stages is as snug as a feather mattress. Only when it hardens does it become uncomfortable."
Maya Angelou

....

....

....

....

....

....

....

....

....

....

....

....

....

....

....

....

....

"Pessimist: One who, when he has the choice of two evils, chooses both."
Oscar Wilde

....

....

....

....

....

....

....

....

....

....

....

....

....

....

....

....

....

....

....

"Action cures fear, inaction creates terror."
Douglas Horton

"It is a very rare man who does not victimize the helpless."
James Baldwin

"Intolerance is the most socially acceptable form of egotism, for it permits us to assume superiority without personal boasting."
Sydney J. Harris

"I've missed more than 9,000 shots in my career. I've lost almost 300 games. Twenty-six times, I've been trusted to take the game-winning shot and missed. I've failed over and over and over again in my life. And that is why I succeed."
Michael Jordan

"Every block of stone has a statue inside it and it is the task of the sculptor to discover it."
Michelangelo

"Never confuse motion with action."
Benjamin Franklin

"Do you want to know who you are? Don't ask. Act! Action will delineate and define you."
Thomas Jefferson

....

....

....

....

....

....

....

....

....

....

....

....

....

....

....

....

....

....

"If you don't like something, change it. If you can't change it, change your attitude."
Maya Angelou

"Time stays long enough for anyone who will use it."
Leonardo da Vinci

"A small body of determined spirits fired by an unquenchable faith in their mission can alter the course of history."
Mahatma Gandhi

"Be who you are and say what you feel, because those who mind don't matter and those who matter don't mind."
Dr. Seuss

"Two people in a conversation amount to four people talking. The four are what one person says, what he really wanted to say, what his listener heard, and what he thought he heard."
William Jennings Bryant

"Let your dreams outgrow the shoes of your expectations."
Ryunosuke Satoro

....

....

....

....

....

....

....

....

....

....

....

....

....

....

....

....

....

....

"Silence can generate feelings of humiliation, anger, resentment that if go unexpressed contaminate every interaction, shut down creativity and undermine productivity."
"Is Silence Killing Your Company?" Harvard Business Review

"If you tell the truth, you don't have to remember anything."
Mark Twain

41
www.leadershipDG.com

"In a controversy the instant we feel anger we have already ceased striving for the truth, and have begun striving for ourselves."
Buddha

"Faith is taking the first step even when you don't see the whole staircase."
Martin Luther King, Jr.

_____

_____

_____

_____

_____

_____

_____

_____

_____

_____

_____

_____

_____

_____

_____

_____

_____

"I don't like that man. I must get to know him better."
Abraham Lincoln

"I learned that courage was not the absence of fear, but the triumph over it.
The brave man is not he who does not feel afraid, but he who conquers that fear."
Nelson Mandela
45
www.leadershipDG.com

"He that is good for making excuses is seldom good for anything else."
Benjamin Franklin

"You aren't learning anything when you're talking."
Lyndon B. Johnson

"Conflict is the beginning of consciousness."
M. Esther Harding

"Intense feeling too often obscures the truth."
Harry S. Truman
49
www.leadershipDG.com

_____

_____

_____

_____

_____

_____

_____

_____

_____

_____

_____

_____

_____

_____

_____

_____

_____

"The best way to find out if you can trust somebody is to trust them."
Ernest Hemingway

"Everything in life is speaking in spite of its apparent silence."
Hazrat Inayat Khan

"Unhappiness is best defined as the difference between our talents and our expectations."
Edward de Bono

"Feedback is the breakfast of champions."
Ken Blanchard

"You don't have to be better than everyone else. You just have to be better than you thought you ever could be."
Ken Venturi

LEADERSHIP
DEVELOPMENT GROUP

"Expect problems and eat them for breakfast."
A. Monapert

"You can never quit. Winners never quit, and quitters never win."
Ted Turner

www.leadershipDG.com

"Don't worry when you are not recognized, but strive to be worthy of recognition."
Abraham Lincoln

"Start NOW, not over."
Jim Peal